J. M. Synge

THE IRISH WRITERS SERIES

James F. Carens, General Editor

TITLE	*AUTHOR*
SEAN O'CASEY	Bernard Benstock
J. C. MANGAN	James Kilroy
W. R. RODGERS	Darcy O'Brien
STANDISH O'GRADY	Phillip L. Marcus
PAUL VINCENT CARROLL	Paul A. Doyle
SEUMAS O'KELLY	George Brandon Saul
SHERIDAN LEFANU	Michael Begnal
AUSTIN CLARKE	John Jordan
BRIAN FRIEL	D. E. S. Maxwell
DANIEL CORKERY	George Brandon Saul
EIMAR O'DUFFY	Robert Hogan
MERVYN WALL	Robert Hogan
FRANK O'CONNOR	James Matthews
GEORGE MOORE	Janet Egleson
JAMES JOYCE	Fritz Senn
JOHN BUTLER YEATS	Douglas Archibald
LORD EDWARD DUNSANY	Zack Bowen
MARIA EDGEWORTH	James Newcomer
MARY LAVIN	Zack Bowen
OSCAR WILDE	Edward Partridge
SOMERVILLE AND ROSS	John Cronin
SUSAN L. MITCHELL	Richard M. Kain
J. M. SYNGE	Robin Skelton
KATHARINE TYNAN	Marilyn Gaddis Rose
LIAM O'FLAHERTY	James O'Brien
IRIS MURDOCH	Donna Gerstenberger
JAMES STEPHENS	Brigit Bramsback
BENEDICT KIELY	Daniel Casey
EDWARD MARTYN	Robert Christopher
BRENDAN BEHAN	John Stewart Collis
DOUGLAS HYDE	Gareth Dunleavy
EDNA O'BRIEN	Grace Eckley
CHARLES LEVER	M. S. Elliott
BRIAN MOORE	Jeanne Flood
SAMUEL BECKETT	Clive Hart
ELIZABETH BOWEN	Edwin J. Kenney
JOHN MONTAGUE	Frank Kersnowski
ROBERT MATURIN	Robert E. Lougy
GEORGE FITZMAURICE	Arthur E. McGuinness
MICHAEL MCCLAVERTY	Leo F. McNamara
FRANCIS STUART	J. H. Natterstad
PATRICK KAVANAGH	Darcy O'Brien
BRINSLEY MACNAMARA AND GEORGE SHIELS	Raymond J. Porter
STEPHEN MACKENNA	Roger Rosenblatt
JACK B. YEATS	Robin Skelton
WILLIAM ALLINGHAM	Alan Warner
SAMUEL LOVER	Mabel Worthington
FLANN O'BRIEN	Bernard Benstock
DENIS JOHNSTON	James F. Carens
WILLIAM LARMINIE	Richard J. Finneran

J. M. SYNGE

Robin Skelton

LEWISBURG
BUCKNELL UNIVERSITY PRESS

© 1972 by Associated University Presses, Inc.

Library of Congress Cataloging in Publication Data

Associated University Presses, Inc.
Cranbury, New Jersey 08512

Skelton, Robin.
    J. M. Synge.

    (The Irish writers series)
    Bibliography: p.
    1. Synge, John Millington, 1871–1909.
PR5533.S48   822′.9′12   75–126277
ISBN 0–8387–7769–4
ISBN 0–8387–7687–6 (pbk)
Printed in the United States of America

Contents

Chronology

1871: J.M. Synge born at 2 Newtown Villas, Rathfarnham, near Dublin, on 16 April.

1872: Synge's father dies. The family moves to 4 Orwell Park, Rathgar.

1886: Synge joins the Dublin Naturalists' Field Club.

1887: He commences studying the violin with Patrick Griffith in Dublin.

1888: He passes the Entrance Examination for Trinity College, Dublin.

1889: He attends lectures in Musical Theory at the Royal Academy of Music.

1890: The Synge family moves to Crosthwaite Park, Kingstown, (now Dun Laoghaire).

1891: Synge joins the Orchestra of the Academy and plays in its March concert.

1892: He receives a pass degree from Trinity College, Dublin.

1893: Synge's first publication. His sonnet *Glencullen* is published in *Kottabos*. He falls in love with Cherry Matheson. He visits Germany to continue his musical studies at Oberwerth, near Coblenz.

1894: He moves from Oberwerth to Wurzburg. After a summer in Ireland he gives up his musical studies and travels to Paris, via Oberwerth. He decides to study at the Sorbonne, while teaching English and working on his writings.

1895: Attends lectures by the anarchist Sebastien Fauré in Paris, and during the summer in Ireland studies Irish antiquities, the Irish Language, and Italian.

1896: He visits Rome and Florence, and at the end of the year in Paris meets W. B. Yeats for the first time.

1897: Joins the Irish League on its foundation in Paris on New Years Day, but resigns from it in April. Studies mysticism and the occult. His hair begins to fall out and he has an operation for a growth in his neck in December at the Mount Street Nursing Home, Dublin.

1898: He visits the Aran Islands for the first time, and on returning to the mainland visits Lady Gregory at Coole. His review of Maeterlinck's *La Sagessse et la Destinée* is published in the *Daily Express,* Dublin.

1899: He visits the Aran Islands for the second time. The Irish Literary Theatre begins its career with a production of Edward Martyn's *The Heather Field* and W. B. Yeats's *The Countess Cathleen.*

1900: Third visit to Aran.

1901: He completes a two-act version of his first play, *When the Moon Has Set,* and *The Aran Islands,* after his fourth visit to the Islands. *The Aran*

Islands is rejected for publication by Grant Richards.

1902: He writes *Luasnad, Capa, and Laine, Vernal Play, Riders to the Sea, In the Shadow of the Glen,* and begins work on *The Tinkers Wedding.* He visits Aran for the last time. The Irish National Theatre Society is founded.

1903: Visits West Kerry for the first time. *Riders to the Sea* is published in the September issue of *Samhain. In the Shadow of the Glen* is first performed on 8 October.

1904: *Riders to the Sea* is first performed on 25 February, and presented in London, together with *In the Shadow of the Glen,* on 26 March. On 20 August *The Abbey Theatre* comes into being. Synge visits Mayo for the first time. *In the Shadow of the Glen* is published in the December issue of *Samhain,* and in a limited edition of fifty copies in New York.

1905: First production of *The Well of the Saints* on 4 February. Molly Allgood joins *The Abbey Theatre* company. Synge visits Connemara and Mayo with Jack B. Yeats and the resultant illustrated articles are published in *The Manchester Guardian.* The Irish National Theatre Society Ltd is created, with Yeats, Lady Gregory, and Synge as Directors. Elkin Mathews publishes *Riders to the Sea* and *The Shadow of the Glen* as one volume of his *Vigo Cabinet* series. *The Well of the Saints* is published by Bullen in London and John Quinn in New York.

1906: Synge falls in love with Molly Allgood. He trans-
lates a selection of Petrarch's sonnets and completes *The Playboy of the Western World.*

1907: *The Playboy of the Western World* is first performed on 26 January, and is published by Maunsel & Co. *The Aran Islands* is published by Elkin
Mathews. Synge is again operated on for a growth
in his neck. The operation is successful, but at
the end of the year Synge begins to experience
pains in his side.

1908: *The Tinkers Wedding* is published by Maunsel
& Co. Exploratory surgery reveals an inoperable
tumor in Synge's side. He visits Germany and,
while there, hears of his mother's death. He completes the text of his volume of *Poems and Translations.*

1909: 24 March. The death of J. M. Synge. *Poems and
Translations* published by the Cuala Press.

1910: *Deirdre of the Sorrows* first performed on 13
January, with Molly Allgood directing and in the
title role. *The Works of John M. Synge* published
in four volumes by Maunsel & Co.

Introduction

John Millington Synge is generally regarded as a playwright whose most important works, *Riders to the Sea* and *The Playboy of the Western World*, gave fresh dignity and depth to the portrayal of the Irish character upon the stage and dealt the death-blow to the stock figure of the "stage Irishman" beloved of comedy writers from the seventeenth century onwards. Together with Lady Gregory, Douglas Hyde, and, later, such lesser dramatists as T. C. Murray and Lennox Robinson, he showed the dramatic possibilities of themes derived from the life of the Irish peasant who had previously been regarded as a subject fit only for mirth. His vigorous and frequently sardonic treatment of his material led to his plays being condemned by many contemporary Irish critics as denigrations of the Irish character, but also led to the creation of much later drama of importance, especially that of George FitzMaurice and Sean O'Casey. His observations of the Irish countryfolk in his book *The Aran Islands* and in his essays led to a renewed interest in native customs and culture; in this they were at one with those works of

Lady Gregory, Douglas Hyde, and W. B. Yeats which drew attention to the richness of Irish folklore, and with the attempts of the poet and economist AE (George Russell) to improve the lot of the Irish peasant. His poems, though few in number, exerted a considerable influence upon the work of W. B. Yeats, and thus upon numerous later poets of the English speaking world.

His work proved to be not only important in itself, but also seminal and far-reaching in its influence upon both Irish and European literature. Nevertheless, although everything he published in his lifetime appeared to be intended to affect the public's attitude towards the problems and glories of his country, and much of his prose and drama has obviously polemic intentions, he once told Padraic Colum that all his work was subjective and came out of moods in his own life.

That life began on 16 April 1871 in 2 Newtown Villas, Rathfarnham, near Dublin. His father, John Hatch Synge, was a lawyer, and a member of a family that had been prominent in Ireland since the seventeenth century, when the first Synge entered the country as a Protestant Bishop. Substantial landowners since 1765 when they intermarried with the wealthy Hatch family, the Synges retained their Protestant faith over the centuries, and during the nineteenth century intensified and narrowed it with an admixture of extreme evangelism.

Synge's mother was particularly zealous in her religion; the daughter of a bigoted puritanical rector, she thought popery, playgoing, and peasant agitation all equally works of the devil. Widowed in 1872, she brought up her children—Robert, Edward, Annie, Samuel, and John—as firm believers in Landlordism, Established Religion, and the British Crown. Only her youngest child reacted against this teaching. Robert became a landowner, Edward a land agent, Samuel a missionary, and Annie the wife of a conservatively minded lawyer. John, however, after reading Darwin in his teens, first doubted, then abandoned orthodox Christianity, and after showing intense interest in ornithology and botany became devoted to the study of music. He studied the violin under Patrick Griffith in Dublin, and also worked at the Royal College of Music while proceeding towards an indifferent B.A. at Trinity College, Dublin. After graduation he studied music further in Germany, but in 1894 he decided to abandon music and turn to literature for a career. He then went to live in Paris where, with the aid of an allowance and some earnings from teaching English, he lived on and off for several years. There he became interested both in politics and folklore, attending lectures at the Sorbonne; there, in 1896, he met W. B. Yeats.

It was apparently Yeats who advised him to return to Ireland and to visit Aran. He made his first trip to Aran in 1898, and visited it again in four successive years. These visits led to his writing *The Aran Islands,* his first mature work. It was not until 1902, however, that he began the series of plays which made him famous. In that year he wrote *Riders to the Sea* and *In the Shadow of the Glen,* and began work on *The Tinker's Wedding.* The Irish National Theatre Society produced *In the Shadow of the Glen* on 8 October 1903 in The Molesworth Hall, Dublin. The play immediately became a source of controversy, for it struck many Irish Nationalists—including, notably, Arthur Griffith—as a libel upon the Irish character in general and Irish womanhood in particular.

Synge, however, had now become a writer of national significance, and from this time forward his life was devoted entirely to his writing and to working in the theatre. *Riders to the Sea* was first performed in Dublin on 25 February 1904, and in March together with *In the Shadow of the Glen* at the Royalty Theatre London, where it was received with acclamation. *The Well of the Saints,* which Synge wrote in the years 1903–04, was produced on 4 February 1905, and regarded by the zealots of Irish nationalism as un-Irish. This view of Synge as a libeller of his native land received its most intense expression, however, on 26 January 1907 when *The Playboy of the Western World* was performed at the Abbey Theatre, and caused riots. Synge had written the play over the years 1904–06, and the heroine, Pegeen Mike, was intended, after the spring of 1905, as a vehicle for the young actress Molly Allgood, with whom he had fallen in love. The *Playboy* riots caused him much discomfort. In 1897 he had suffered an operation on his neck for a swollen gland, the first indications of the presence of Hodgkins Disease. Now, weakened by emotional exhaustion, he fell ill again though he was well enough to attend the first London performance of *Playboy* on 8 June 1907 at the Great Queen Street Theatre, where it was a resounding success. However he had by now become distrustful of the Abbey Theatre's cautious treatment of his plays, and their refusal to perform *Playboy* in Birmingham on that 1907 tour upset him greatly.

The Tinker's Wedding, which he completed in 1907, was regarded as too dangerous to be performed in Ireland, and was indeed first produced after its author's death by the Afternoon Theatre Company at His Majesty's Theatre, London, on 11 November 1909. In 1907 *The Aran Islands* was published, and in 1908 Synge was obliged to go into hospital for an exploratory operation to discover the cause of pains in his side. An inoperable tumor was discovered. He had already begun writing *Deirdre of the Sorrows,* and had completed work on a small book of poems. Now, in his last months, he tried to finish this new play, intended from the first as a vehicle for Molly. He never did complete it, however. He died on 24 March 1909. A complete version was assembled from the typescripts by W. B. Yeats and Molly Allgood, and the play was performed on 13 January 1910, with Molly as director and as Deirdre. During that year the *Collected Works* of J. M. Synge were published in four volumes by Maunsel of Dublin, but, with the exception of a few notebook passages published in 1932, the whole of Synge's work was not to appear in print until 1962–68 when Oxford University Press published a definitive edition. This edition presented much new material, including many poems, much early prose and several fragments of drama. It has not been until very recently, therefore, that it has become possible to qualify the popular view of Synge derived from his major works with a deeper understanding of his career based upon the study of his worksheets, his early writings, and his notebooks.

All quotations in this essay are taken from the Oxford University Press edition of the *Works.*

J. M. Synge

I

Synge's earliest known piece of sustained writing was a nature diary which he wrote in collaboration with his cousin Florence Ross at the age of ten. Poetry occupied him somewhat during his student days and an early sonnet was published in the Trinity College magazine *Kottabos,* for the Hilary Term 1893. It was not until he settled in Paris, however, that he began seriously to tackle literary production. At this time all his work was related directly to his own personal experiences. He kept notebooks in which he recorded his thoughts and described those childhood experiences which he felt to have been most influential. He identified several emotional crises. The first concerned his early experience of the notion of Hell.

> I was painfully timid, and while still very young the idea of Hell took a fearful hold on me. One night I thought I was irretrievably damned and cried myself to sleep in vain yet terrified efforts to form a conception of eternal pain. In the morning I renewed my lamentations and my mother was sent for. She comforted me with the assurance that the Holy Ghost was convicting me of sin and thus preparing me for ultimate salvation. This was a new idea,

and I rather approved. [A notebook of 1896–98. *Works*
II.4.]

The second concerned an early experience of rejection.
His childish but intense affection for his cousin Florence was at first returned, but in 1882 she became
temporarily much more interested in another boy.
Synge wrote of his being "stunned with horror" and
described how he "fretted myself ill in lonely corners,
whistling 'Down in Alabama,' the only love-song I
knew." Trivial though this experience may seem, it was
for him, as a young man, significant; it had proved to
be only the first of a series of rejections by girls to whom
he became emotionally attached.

It was his reading of Darwin at approximately the
age of fourteen, however, which produced what he
clearly regarded as the most intense crisis.

> When I was about fourteen I obtained a book of Darwin's.
> It opened in my hands at a passage where he asks how can
> we explain the similarity between a man's hand and a
> bird's or bat's wings except by evolution. I flung the book
> aside and rushed out into the open air—it was summer and
> we were in the country—the sky seemed to have lost its blue
> and the grass its green. I lay down and writhed in an agony
> of doubt. My studies showed me the force of what I read,
> [and] the more I put it from me the more it rushed back
> with new instances and power. I had never doubted and
> never conceived that a sane and wise man or boy could
> doubt. I had of course heard of atheists but as vague mon-
> sters that I was unable to realize. It seemed that I was be-
> come in a moment the playfellow of Judas. Incest and par-
> ricide were but a consequence of the idea that possessed
> me. [A notebook of 1896–98. II 10.]

This experience led to his renouncing Christianity

altogether, and he wrote, "laid a chasm between my
present and my past and between myself and my kin-
dred and friends. Till I was twenty-three I never met
or at least knew a man or woman who shared my
opinions." He satisfied his religious needs by adopting
a form of nature mysticism which fitted in with his
already intense interest in the natural world. He could
not, however, solve the problem of alienation from
his family faith so easily. When he fell in love with
Cherry Matheson, the daughter of a leader of the
Plymouth brethren, he faced rejection again, and this
time on account of his atheism rather than because of
outside competition. This rejection, together with similar difficulties with other girls, provided him with the
impetus to write his first completed work. Entitled
Vita Vecchia it was written in Paris in 1895–97, and
consisted of a series of poems linked together by a
fictional narrative in the form of a journal. The poems
are all filled with hectic despair, and express their supposed writer's rejection of all hope, and even his
decision not to have children in case they should be as
sickly as he—a decision to which Synge himself had
come as a boy in a period of more than usually intense
melancholy.

Vita Vecchia was followed by another and more
elaborate work, *Etude Morbide,* also in journal form.
This again reflects Synge's own preoccupations; it in-
cludes reflections upon religion, passages of near-
mysticism, celebrations of the simple dignity of peasant
life in Brittany (which Synge had just visited), and a
portrayal of the violinist hero's agony at the failure of
his musical ambitions, as well as much tortured con-

templation of his relationship with the two women in his life. Synge later dismissed this work as "morbid" and said that he hated it. It is, however, valuable to us in showing how he was attempting, in his early twenties, to heal psychic scars by means of his writing and to come to some philosophical conclusions about human existence.

Passages from these two early journals occur in early drafts of Synge's first completed play, *When the Moon Has Set*. This he began in 1896–98 in Paris. He had completed a two-act version by 1901 when he showed it to Yeats and Lady Gregory, and then revised it further, completing a one-act version in May 1903. Although it is clearly a very bad play indeed in all its versions, it was of sufficient personal importance for him to continue working on it even after he had achieved the mature drama of *Riders to the Sea* and *In the Shadow of the Glen*.

It is easy to see why he found it important. The plot is simple. In esssence it tells of a young man persuading a nun, his late uncle's nurse, to abandon her calling and marry him. He uses as an argument the experience of an old woman he has met who in her youth rejected his uncle's proposal on the advice of priests, and thereafter went mad. The uncle, like Synge, had been rejected "because he did not believe in God." Obviously Synge was, in this play, dramatizing his feelings towards Cherry Matheson, whom his German friends on hearing of her recalcitrance had nicknamed "The Holy One." Early drafts of the play contain much of Synge's own philosophy. The hero says at one point:

The only calm of importance is the calm of the man who
feels the vortex of passion and death straining beneath
him and is able to deride it. . . . The world is a mode of
the Divine exaltation and every sane fragment of force
ends in a fertile passion that is filled with joy. It is the
infertile excitements that are filled with death. That is
the whole moral and aesthetic of the world. [III 168]

And in another place:

The worst vice is slight compared with the guiltiness of
a man or woman who defies the central order of the
world. . . . The only truth a wave knows is that it is going
to break. The only truth a bud knows is that it is going to
expand and flower. The only truth we know is that we are
a flood of magnificent life the fruit of some frenzy of the
earth. . . . The European races may be swept away,
humanity itself may die out, but a turmoil of life is within
us. It has come from eternity and I suppose it will go on
for eternity. [III 168]

Synge uses music as an image several times in these
early works, and in one draft of *When the Moon Has
Set* he wrote a paragraph which expresses one of the
central concerns of his mature drama.

Every life is a symphony. It is this cosmic element in the
person which gives all personal art, and all sincere life,
and all passionate love a share in the dignity of the
world. . . . If art is the expression of the abstract beauty
of the person there are times when the person is the expression of the beauty that is beyond the world. [III 176]

This passage was written in 1901 and may recall an
essay Synge wrote after he had been operated on for the
removal of a swollen gland in his neck in December
1897. On recovering from being anaesthetized he had a

dream in which he appeared to "travel whole epochs of desolation and bliss." "All secrets," he wrote, "were open before me, and simple as the universe to its God." The dream faded shortly after he had begun to wake fully but then, after a day of rest, he found himself observing things around him with an unusual intensity.

> I took notice of every familiar occurrence as if it were something I had come back to from a distant country. The impression was very strong on me that I had died the preceding day and come to life again, and this impression has never changed. [II 43.]

This experience appears to have been crucial in Synge's development. It was in the summer of 1898, after he had recovered from his operation, that he first set foot on Aran and immediately began another journal, which, unlike *Vita Vecchia* and *Etude Morbide,* was undisguisedly autobiographical, and which served as a quarry from which he extracted themes, settings, and characters for his plays.

The Aran Islands does indeed have that almost hallucinatory intensity of vision which Synge experienced after his operation, and though he maintained in a prefatory note that he had "given a direct account of my life on the islands, and of what I met with among them, inventing nothing and changing nothing that is essential," it is immediately noticeable that he is as much concerned with his own inner life, his own emotional discoveries, as with the social scene before him. He mentions few of the antiquities of the island, though he studied the subject as a student in Trinity, and he refers to earlier visitors in a passage which reveals his emotional commitment to Aran.

> With this limestone Inishmaan however I am in love, and hear with galling jealousy of the various priests and scholars who have lived here before me. They have grown to me as the former lover of one's mistress, horrible existences haunting with dreamed kisses the lips she presses to your own." [II. 103]

This is not guidebook stuff. It is autobiographical confession, and though Synge excised this passage from his finished work he left in sufficient similar material to make it impossible for any unprejudiced reader to regard the book as an objective record.

Synge found the heroic in Aran. He dwelt long upon the wildness of the peasants, and upon their simplicity and courage. He detected in their stories the presence of ancient myths, and suspected in their superstitions traces of pre-Christian belief. He noted how on Inishmor,

> These strange men with receding foreheads, high cheekbones, and ungovernable eyes seem to represent some old type found on these few acres at the extreme border of Europe, where it is only in wild jests and laughter that they can express their loneliness and desolation. [II 140]

This desolation and solitude he found almost epic and, in describing the keen over the grave of an old woman, said,

> The grief of the keen is no personal complaint for the death of one woman over eighty years, but seems to contain the whole passionate rage that lurks somewhere in

every native of the island. In this cry of pain the inner consciousness of the people seems to lay itself bare for an instant, and to reveal the mood of beings who feel their isolation in the face of a universe that wars on them with winds and seas. [II 75]

His own vision becomes more mythic as the book proceeds, and the writing becomes more subjective. Talking of the islanders, he tells us that

There is hardly an hour I am with them that I do not feel the shock of some inconceivable idea, and then again the shock of some vague emotion that is familiar to them and to me. [II 113]

The men of Inishmaan he finds "moved by strange archaic sympathies with the world" and he thinks their life "perhaps the most primitive that is left in Europe." He sees in the domestic articles on Aran "an almost personal character which gives this simple life, where all art is unknown, something of the artistic beauty of medieval life" and suggests that the harshness of the environment "makes it impossible for clumsy, foolhardy, or timid men" to live there. Preferring this "primitive" life to modern society, he suggests that

It is likely that much of the intelligence and charm of these people is due to the absence of any division of labour, and to the correspondingly wide development of each individual, whose varied knowledge and skill necessitates a considerable activity of mind. [II. 132]

These people, because of the way in which their lives have never been acted on by anything artificial,

seem in a certain sense to approach more nearly to the

finer type of our aristocracies—who are bred artificially to a natural ideal—than to the labourer or citizen, as the wild horse resembles the thoroughbred rather than the hack or cart-horse. [II 66]

It was not only the wildness, reserve, intelligence, charm and natural aristocracy of the islanders that attracted him in Aran. It was also the way in which they seemed possessed of a racial memory that made their stories echo many of the themes and figures of European myth and epic. He felt that there might be "a psychic memory attached to certain neighbourhoods" and that for him his cottage on Aran might well be one.

Synge found on Aran a life completely opposed to that middle-class gentility in which he had been brought up and from which he had alienated himself. He found also a way of life that appealed to those anarchist sympathies he had discovered in himself at the lectures of the anarchist Sébastien Fauré, and an awareness of the supernatural and mythic that appealed to his interest in the world of the psychic and occult which he had also investigated in Paris. It was as if in Aran he had found an "objective correlative" for his own emotional and psychological needs and beliefs, and it was, perhaps, this subjective involvement with the islands that made the stories he heard there powerful enough for him to be compelled to extend them into drama.

The first plays that he wrote after his Aran experience were not, however, based upon direct observation. He began 1902 by writing two plays in verse. The first, the *Vernal Play*, which now exists as fragments, is only of interest in revealing how he attempted to present an idyllic pastoral setting for themes of love and death in a language which could include both "literary" and "folk" elements. Thus we have a sentence by Boinn which begins with a literary use of the word "stores" and ends with a common colloquial locution

> Sycamores
> And larch and birch and sallows breathe new stores
> The time the rain is falling and it warm
> The way it's falling this day, [III. 190]

The second play, *Luasnad Capa and Laine,* is more clearly related both to Synge's emotional situation at the time and to his experiences on Aran. It concerns the three fisherman, Luasnad, Capa, and Laine, who, with their wives, come to Ireland from Spain and settle there, only to be destroyed in the Deluge. Here the language is harsh, direct, even brutal. Luasnad and Capa hear a cry from the women:

CAPA: Your wife is still in labour?
LUASNAD: When women do good things they choose a
               time
               That makes it silly. Here the child will die. [III
               196]

Later we have the exchange:

LAINE: Your child is born Luasnad, and it lives.
CAPA: It is the first man's child has cried on Banba.
LUASNAD: It will be the first dead human body.
               Count the hills.
LAINE: Lugdubh,
               Craigmoira, Tonagee and Inchavor.
LUASNAD: Three are covered?
LAINE: And the rest are sinking. [III. 197]

The incantatory use of proper names combines with the harshness and directness of the language to create real poignancy. When only Luasnad and Laine's wife are left alive, we are given a picture of the gods wreaking destruction upon man only in order to escape the wearisome repetition of human prayers. Luasnad tells us:

> All this life has been a hurtful game
> Played out by steps of anguish. Every beast
> Is bred with fearful torment in the womb
> And bred by fearful torments in life-blood.
> Yet by a bait of love the aimless gods
> Have made us multitudes. [III. 200]

Nevertheless the "bait of love" cannot be ignored, and in primitive and passionate assertion of the dignity of the individual human's needs Luasnad makes love to Laine's wife as the waters rise towards them. He feels that they are only one small part of that "turmoil of life" which is creation and which exists as unity.

> Dead men pass.　　There lives
> Only one life, one passion of one love,
> One world wind sea, then one deep dream of death.
> 　　　　　　　　　　　　　[III. 204]

Man can, however, achieve "a share in the dignity of the world" by asserting, however fruitlessly, his individuality and thus embodying the very power that created and empowers the gods themselves,

Man's last high mood
Can pass above this passion of the seas
That moans to crush him. In each man's proper joy
The first high puissance that made live the gods
Lives on the earth and asks the stone for worship.

[III. 205]

Luasnad Capa and Laine is epic in theme and tragic
in intensity, though all we now have are two fragments
of it. It derives from Synge's observation of the laments
of the Aran peasants in the face of their harsh life and
inevitable doom; and it also derives from his own
agonized childhood terror of death, his distrust of religion, and the despair and frustration of his personal
life. Now, however, what was merely transcribed into
fiction in the *Etude Morbide* journal, and what was
further "distanced" by the seemingly more objective
account in the Aran book, has become entirely objecti-
fied into drama. Synge completed *Luasnad Capa and
Laine* in the early months of 1902 in Paris. On his return to Ireland he began work on *Riders to the Sea*.

II

The plot of *Riders to the Sea* derives from two passages in *The Aran Islands*. In the first we are told of a drowned man whose identity can only be established by a close scrutiny of his clothing. At last the sister of a man missing from the island

> . . . pieced together all she could remember about his clothes, and what his purse was like, and where he had got it, and the same of his tobacco box, and his stockings. In the end there seemed little doubt that it was her brother. "Ah!" she said, "it's Mike sure enough, and please God they'll give him a decent burial." [II. 136]

The play opens with two sisters, Cathleen and Nora, examining the clothing of a drowned man to see if it is that of their brother Michael. The second passage provided Synge with the second thread of his plot.

> When the horses were coming down to the slip an old woman saw her son, that was drowned a while ago, riding on one of them. She didn't say what she was after seeing, and this man caught the horse, he caught his own horse first, and then he caught this one, and after that he went out and was drowned. [II. 164]

When Maurya goes out to see her son Bartley off and to give him her blessing, she sees the spectre of Michael riding behind him. She is unable to give her blessing, and Bartley is drowned. The old woman has now lost all her menfolk to the sea.

It is a simple plot, and one with obvious possibilities of pathos. Synge, however, chose to do more than retell a story of human loss and grief. Firstly, he incorporated into the play many images with supernatural significance, so that the events of the drama take place against a back-cloth, not of the physical Aran only, but also of the world of the spirit. Thus there are references to Samhain (or Hallowe'en) the time when ghosts walk, to holy water, and to "the black hags" that "do be flying on the sea." Maurya meets Bartley and Michael's spectre down by the "spring well," a location associated with the supernatural in numerous stories. Michael's body is found by the "black cliffs": such dark cliffs are associated in myths of many lands with the idea of death and the entrance to the underworld. The sea itself is regarded as a godlike power in the play, and the priest is dismissed as being of very little significance. Moreover, the way in which Bartley's death follows Maurya's finding herself unable to give him her blessing reminds one of the way in which the drowning of Hippolitus is caused by his mother's anger at his rejecting her incestuous love.

The language of the play emphasizes these elements of the mythic and epic. Though the vocabulary is simple, the cadences are stately, and the statements of Maurya at the end of the play have that elemental and primitive quality which one associates equally with the deepest feelings and the most heroic of ancient poetry.

They're all gone now, and there isn't anything more the
sea can do to me. . . . I'll have no call now to be up
crying and praying when the wind breaks from the south,
and you can hear the surf is in the east, and the surf is in
the west, making a great stir with the two noises, and they
hitting one on the other. I'll have no call now to be going
down and getting Holy Water in the dark nights after
Samhain, and I won't care what way the sea is when the
other women will be keening. . . . It isn't that I haven't
prayed for you, Bartley, to the Almighty God. It isn't that
I haven't said prayers in the dark night till you wouldn't
know what I'd be saying; but it's a great rest I'll have
now, and it's time surely. It's a great rest I'll have now,
and great sleeping in the long nights after Samhain, if
it's only a bit of wet flour we do have to eat, and maybe a
fish that would be stinking. [III. 23 & 25]

The combination in this speech of incantatory repetition, simple language, allusions to vast spiritual
powers, and, at the end, down-to-earth particularities,
gives it both tragic stature and human poignancy.

It is the particularity of much of the language which
frees *Riders to the Sea* from that sentimental inflation
which vitiates so much nineteenth-century domestic
drama. The talk is of simple things: of the ladder that
must be moved to reach the turf loft, of the cake baking
at the fire, of the pig with black feet, and of the small
details of cottage life. Moreover, the simplicity and
limited nature of the islanders' experience is empha-
sized over and over again by the use of local detail. The
ship is described as "passing the green head"; footsteps
are heard passing "the big stones"; the stick is identified
as "the stick Michael brought from Connemara"; the
world of the play is one in which poverty and custom

together make every smallest thing of significance, almost, as Synge said in *The Aran Islands,* giving each
article a "personal life."

This world is contrasted several times with the world
outside it. When Maurya takes the dead Michael's
stick to help her to the spring to meet Bartley and give
him her blessing, she says

> In the big world the old people do be leaving things after
> them for their sons and children, but in this place it is the
> young men do be leaving things behind for them that do
> be old. [III. 13]

The thing that has been left is no more than a stick.
The way in which the smallest objects have deep significance and value in this land is also, by implication,
contrasted with the attitudes of the big world. The final
indication that Maurya has now lost all grip upon life
is made by means of a packet of nails.

CATHLEEN: Maybe yourself and Eamon would make
               a coffin when the sun rises. We have fine
               white boards herself bought, God help her,
               thinking Michael would be found, and I
               have a new cake you can eat while you'll
               be working.

THE OLD MAN: Are there nails with them?

CATHLEEN: There are not, Colum; we didn't think of
               the nails.

ANOTHER MAN: It's a great wonder she wouldn't think of
               the nails, and all the coffins she's seen
               made already.

CATHLEEN: It's getting old she is, and broken. [III 25]

Synge was not, in *Riders to the Sea,* concerned only
to portray the life on Aran, and to indicate how in that

place the people, faced by an unrelenting sea, call as
often upon pre-Christian as Christian belief, and create
a world of passionate significance from those few elements of their household and their environment to
which they can attach memories and values. He was
also concerned, as in all his plays, to comment upon
the human predicament itself. In *Riders to the Sea* the
deaths do not occur, as in Shakespearean tragedy, as the
consequence of some "fatal flaw" in the characters, or
even, as in Euripides, as the consequence of a sin against
Divine Law. There may be a touch of suggested causal-
ity in the death of Bartley following his mother's with-
holding of her blessing, but, basically, the tragedy of
the play is the arbitrariness of the suffering and death
imposed. Moreover Maurya, at its close, does not rail
against the gods or God or the fates. Nor does she make
the claim made at the close of so many tragedies that
somehow the whole affair can be seen as ennobling the
image of man. She does not glorify the memories of her
dead. She asks little, and the little she asks is what she
herself can provide.

> Michael has a clean burial in the far north, by the grace
> of the Almighty God. Bartley will have a fine coffin out of
> the white boards, and a deep grave surely. . . . What more
> can we want than that? No man at all can be living for
> ever, and we must be satisfied. [III 27]

In this she contrasts with the old woman of Yeats's
play, *Cathleen ni Houlihan,* which was first performed
in April 1902 and published later the same year, at the
time when Synge was writing *Riders to the Sea.* Her
last words are

They shall be remembered for ever,
They shall be alive for ever,
They shall be speaking for ever.
The people shall hear them for ever.

Riders to the Sea and *Cathleen ni Houlihan* are
similar in several respects. Both plays are set in a cottage; both involve at an early stage the examination of
clothing; both present an old woman keening over the
death of young men of whom she has been fond; and
both are concerned primarily with the fate of a young
man called Michael. The contrasts are as interesting as
the similarities. Yeats's Michael awaits his wedding, and
Synge's Michael his funeral. Yeats's young men run to
the sea to join the French fleet; Synge's Bartley rides
down to the sea to go to a horse fair. Yeats's old woman
was, of course, the Shan Van Vocht, a personification
of Ireland, and her last words prophesy immortality
for those Irishmen killed in the fight for Irish Freedom;
Synge's Maurya does not seem to be so allegorical a
figure. And yet, if one recognizes the similarity between Synge's play and Yeats's, one is forced to wonder
if Synge was not, by allusion, seeking to indicate that
Maurya might also be regarded as the Shan Van Vocht,
and Aran, isolated from the "big world," as an Ireland
battered and wrenched by forces which the inhabitants
cannot control and whose life-and-death decisions appear to them to be arbitrary decisions of the fates.

It would, perhaps, be wrong to regard *Riders to the
Sea* as allegorical in this sense. It would also, however,
be wrong entirely to dismiss this allegorical approach,
for Maurya clearly represents not merely the Aran

peasant, but also the Irish peasant trapped between two cultures—the ancient pre-Christian one and the new one of the priests and bishops. She is as culturally confused, one might say, as the many peasants Synge described in Aran and in the glens of Wicklow. She holds to the old ways, getting Holy water from the pagan well, and believing in the efficacy of the old blessings, yet finds herself referring constantly to the spiritual world in terms of the Christian "Almighty God."

It is this cultural confusion, or conflict, which Synge found in Aran, and used in *Riders to the Sea,* that became a major theme of his later plays. It is present in all of them save *Deirdre of the Sorrows,* and most powerfully in the two other plays he was working on in 1902, *In the Shadow of the Glen* and *The Tinker's Wedding.* In his perception of this aspect of Irish peasant life Synge is clearly being at once more objective than Yeats and, from another point of view, more subjective also. He is not, like Yeats in *Cathleen ni Houlihan* or *The Countess Cathleen,* simplifying reality in order to make a poetical and polemical point. He is recording the psychological condition of the Irish countryfolk with more accuracy than Yeats ever achieved. On the other hand, it seems clear that in the confusion of cultures he detected in the Aran peasants, and in their poignant attempts to cope with a world beyond their understanding, he found an echo of his own alienation from the Protestant creed of his middle class upbringing, and of his instinctive sympathy with near-mystical pagan beliefs and his feeling for the psychic vitality of the most bare and wild areas of his native land. Moreover, into *Riders to the Sea* he also put his own attempt to come to terms with the notion of mortality, an attempt he had had to make himself as a small child terrified of Hell, and as a young man in 1898 under the surgeon's knife.

It is impossible always to separate an author's private and personal necessities from his more controlled selections of theme and form. We can only point to whatever evidence is available and suggest that one or another deduction may not be entirely wrong. In the case of *Riders to the Sea* it is perhaps enough to suggest that Synge created a peasant drama with the intensity and dignity of a fragment of epic, and that in Maurya he portrayed a figure of wracked and grieving motherhood so absolutely convincing and so universal in its application that it can stand not only for Ireland but for all countries and for all mothers who, in their simplicity and passionate fears and affections, find themselves bereaved of their children by a force they cannot understand, whether it be labelled the Atlantic Ocean, the English Conqueror, or the War in Vietnam.

III

In the Shadow of the Glen, like *Riders to the Sea,*
deals with people isolated from the "big world." Im-
prisoned by what John Butler Yeats called, in a comment on the play, "our Irish institution, the loveless
marriage," and by the solitude of her life in the Wicklow glens, Nora Burke has long been rebelling secretly
against her lot. When her old husband dies, the tramp,
who finds her alone with the corpse, is astonished at
her comparative equanimity. When she leaves him to
go out and give the news to neighbors, however, the
dead man sits up and explains that he has only pre-
tended to be dead in order to catch his wife with her
lover. When Nora returns with Michael Dara, the old
man has his wish. Nora is turned out of the house to
travel the roads.

This simple tale, which Synge adapted from one
heard on Aran, is of the stuff of farce. It reminds one
(as Synge's critics were quick to point out) of the
story of the Widow of Ephesus in Petronius's *Satyricon,*
and in its general structure it reminds one also of many
of the bawdy stories of Boccaccio. Aware of the story

as one current for many centuries in Europe, and also of its previous use for purposes of broad comedy, Synge chose to make it intensely local in feeling, and almost tragic in its implications. He indicated with clarity the sexual frustration and hunger of Nora. She says of her husband "he was always cold, every day since I knew him—and every night," and admits her fondness for the dead Patch Darcy. Michael Dara has difficulties in his herding, and tells her:

> "I was destroyed surely. . . . They were that wilful they were running off into one man's bit of oats, and another man's bit of hay, and tumbling into the red bogs till it's more like a pack of old goats than sheep they were. . . . Mountain ewes is a queer breed, Nora Burke, and I'm not used to them at all."

Nora replies

> "There's no one can drive a mountain ewe but the men do be reared in the Glen Malure, I've heard them say, and above by Rathvanna, and the Glen Imaal, men the like of Patch Darcy. . . ." [III 47]

It is easy to see that Nora is one of the mountain ewes Darcy knew how to control and Michael Dara does not, and the comparison of the wild goats with the ewes (goats being noted for lechery) makes the implication clear. Synge was courageous in presenting sexual hunger and promiscuity on the stage at this time, and the more so because he presented them sympathetically. He wrote to Stephen McKenna, who had objected to the play:

> Heaven forbid that we should have a morbid sex obseded drama in Ireland, not because we have any peculiar sanctity which I utterly deny—blessed unripeness is some-

times akin to damned rottenness, see percentage of luna-
tics in Ireland and causes thereof—but because it is bad as
drama and is played out. On [the] French stage you get
sex without its balancing elements: on [the] Irish stage
you get [the] other elements without sex. I restored sex and
the people were so surprised that they saw the sex only. . . .

Among the other elements that the play's first audience
failed to notice was Nora's feeling that she had betrayed
her own high standards by entering into this marriage.

It's in a lonesome place you do have to be talking with
someone, and looking for someone, in the evening of the
day, and if it's a power of men I'm after knowing they
were fine men, for I was a hard child to please, and a hard
girl to please (*she looks at him a little sternly*) and it's a
hard woman I am to please this day, Michael Dara, and
it's no lie, I'm telling you. [III 49]

Her frustration is not sexual only. She longs for the
freedom of the single woman, but fears the poverty and
suffering of such as "Peggy Cavanagh" walking the
roads. She is envious of those of her contemporaries
who have had children, yet when contemplating marriage to Michael Dara she can only think of the horror
of advancing age. She is frustrated as much by time as
by sexual deprivation.

"Why would I marry you, Mike Dara? You'll be getting
old, and I'll be getting old, and in a little while, I'm
telling you, you'll be sitting up in your bed—the way
himself was sitting—with a shake in your face, and your
teeth falling, and the white hair sticking out round you
like an old bush where sheep do be leaving a gap." [III 51]

Nora's awareness of the emotional poverty of her
situation is in sharp contrast to the attitudes of the

menfolk in the play. Her husband dislikes her sensitivity. Michael Dara thinks only of the amount of money she will bring to her marriage and does not propose to her until "five pounds and ten notes" is piled before him on the table. Only the tramp is untainted by masculine materialism, and listens with understanding to the lyrical melancholy of her complaint when she says

> ". . . isn't a dead man itself more company than to be sitting alone, and hearing the winds crying, and you not knowing on what thing your mind would stay?" [III. 41]

When Dan reveals his subterfuge, Nora's immediate reaction is to say "Is it dead he is or living?" and the question suggests that Dan Burke, who has always been "cold," is, whether breathing or not, without emotional life or sensibility. The tramp, on the other hand, is emphatically alive; and it is he who tries to give Nora her dream, telling her

> "Come along with me now, lady of the house, and it's not my blather you'll be hearing only, but you'll be hearing the herons crying out over the black lakes, and you'll be hearing the grouse, and the owls with them, and the larks and the big thrushes when the days are warm, and it's not from the like of them you'll be hearing a talk of getting old like Peggy Cavanagh, and losing the hair off you, and the light of your eyes, but it's fine songs you'll be hearing when the sun goes up, and there'll be no old fellow wheezing the like of a sick sheep close to your ear." [III. 57]

The figure of the tramp is important in Synge's work. In a note written in 1898 he said:

> Man is naturally a nomad . . . and all wanderers have finer intellectual and physical perceptions than men who

are condemned to local habitations. The cycle, automobile and conducted tours are half-conscious efforts to replace the charm of the stage coach and of pilgrimage like Chaucer's. But the vagrant, I think, along with perhaps the sailor, has preserved the dignity of motion with its whole sensation of strange colours in the clouds and of strange passages with voices that whisper in the dark and still stranger inns and lodgings, affections and lonely songs that rest for a whole life time with the perfume of spring evenings or the first autumnal smoulder of the leaves. . . . There is something grandiose in a man who has forced all kingdoms of the earth to yield the tribute of his bread and who, at a hundred, begs on the wayside with the pride of an emperor. The slave and beggar are wiser than the man who works for recompense, for all our moments are divine and above all price though their sacrifice is paid with a measure of fine gold. Every industrious worker has sold his birthright for a mess of pottage, perhaps served him in chalices of gold. . . .
[II 195–196.]

In another notebook of 1907, on meeting some vagrants he commented:

People like these, like the old woman and these two beautiful children, are a precious possession for any country. They console us, one moment at least, for the manifold and beautiful life we have all missed who have been born in modern Europe. . . .   [II 199.]

In such people he saw a life in harmony with the moods of the earth, and therefore also a philosophical attitude far superior to that provided by the conventional beliefs and moral regulations of the church.

The tramp of *In the Shadow of the Glen* is not, however, a heroic figure. Afraid of the supernatural, he is careful to stick a pin under his lapel to repel ghosts, and he recites the De Profundis when left alone with the corpse. He is, however, perceptive, and it is he who brings Nora to her decision by suggesting that Michael Dara might have her after she has been turned out by her husband. Dara has already suggested her going to the "Union below in Rathdrum," a fate that the countryfolk consider much worse than death itself. Nora, understanding the materialism of the young man, says bitterly: "What would he do with me now?"

The tramp's reply is gentle, but it is, in its suggestion of real charity, a terrible indictment of the other man's inhumanity. "Give you the half of a dry bed, and good food in your mouth," he says, and Dan Burke retorts "Is it a fool you think him, stranger, or is it a fool you were born yourself?" The "Christian" beliefs, which provided Dan Burke with justification for turning his adulterous wife out on the roads and which enabled him to contemplate her future suffering with complacency rather than compassion, did not oblige him to regard charity and kindness as anything other than folly.

It is with courage that Nora finally leaves her home for a life of wandering, feeling that at least in her new life there will be "a fine bit of talk," and that she will no longer be lonesome. In that talk she may find a hint of the life of beauty and zest she has desired and been deprived of for so long. Nora Burke is the first of Synge's rebellious dreamers, and perhaps the most bitter one. From this play onwards he was to deal again and again with themes of rejection and rebellion, and with the conflict between the morality of convention and the divine discontent of the passionate human heart.

IV

In a letter to Max Meyerfeld written in 1906, Synge described _The Tinker's Wedding_ as "a little play written before the 'Well of the Saints' but never played here because it is thought too immoral and anti-clerical." He took his plot from a story told him in Wicklow, which he printed in his essay _At a Wicklow Fair_. The story is told him by a herd, referring to a tinker who has passed by:

> "That man is a great villain. . . . One time he and his woman went up to a priest in the hills and asked him would he wed them for half a sovereign, I think it was. The priest said it was a poor price, but he'd wed them surely if they'd make him a tin can along with it. 'I will, faith,' said the tinker, 'and I'll come back when it's done.' They went off then, and in three weeks they came back, and they asked the priest a second time would he wed them. 'Have you the tin can?' said the priest. 'We have not', said the tinker; 'we had it made at the fall of night, but the ass gave it a kick this morning the way it isn't fit for you at all.' 'Go on now,' says the priest. 'It's a pair of rogues and schemers you are, and I won't wed you at all.' They went off then, and they were never married to this day." [II 228]

Synge compressed this story into the space of two

days, and made the old Tinker woman, Mary Byrne, sell the can for drink rather than having it destroyed by an ass. He also, however, created in Sarah Casey another of his rebellious heroines whose passionate imaginations will not allow them to rest. Sarah is in harmony with the earth; she is affected by the arrival of Spring. Since the "changing of the moon" she has acted strangely. She tells Michael "Spring-time is a queer time, and it's queer thoughts maybe I do think at whiles." She sees herself in heroic terms as "the Beauty of Ballinacree" and boasts of the way men follow her "talking love" and of the way children are astonished at her beauty. She longs for the dignity of ritual and sees this in terms of the Christian rites that would make her a conventional bride. Her psychic energy gives rise to both poetry and violence. In the first act she is inclined towards romantic fantasies, but in the second, when her desire for marriage is frustrated, she becomes abusive and yells at the priest who intervenes to stop her attacking Mary,

> "I've bet a power of strong lads east and west through the world, and are you thinking I'd turn back from a priest? Leave the road now, or maybe I would strike yourself." [IV. 43]

The wildness of her imagination is revealed when she tells the Priest, who has threatened to tell the police who was responsible for the theft of Philly Cullen's ass,

> "If you do, you'll be getting all the tinkers from Wicklow and Wexford, and the County Meath, to put up block tin in the place of glass to shield your windows where you do be looking out and blinking at the girls. It's hard set you'll

> be that time, I'm telling you, to fill the depth of your belly the long days of Lent; for we wouldn't leave a laying pullet in your yard at all." [IV. 45]

Nevertheless, her desires are real, and her dream of matrimonial glory is important to her. Magnificently, she tells the priest that if he does not marry her to Michael she will go and complain to the bishop even if it means walking to Dublin "with blood and blisters on my naked feet," thus reminding us of the Christian pilgrims to the holy places of Ireland. In her desire for a Christian sacrament, she is running counter to the traditions of her own people who are here represented by Mary Byrne whose stories are of pagan times,

> of the great queens of Ireland with white necks on them the like of Sarah Cascy, and fine arms would hit you a slap the way Sarah Casey would hit you. [IV. 25]

It is Mary Byrne, and not the priest, who understands Sarah Casey's spiritual condition. It is Mary Byrne who talks to the priest at the close of the play as if he were a poor child or a simpleton; it is she who embodies the wisdom as well as the folly of the play.

> It's sick and sorry we are to tease you; but what did you want meddling with the like of us, when it's a long time we are going our own ways—father and son, and his son after him, or mother and daughter, and her own daughter again—and it's little need we ever had of going up into a church and swearing—I'm told there's swearing with it— a word no man would believe, or with drawing rings on our fingers, would be cutting our skins maybe when we'd be taking the ass from the shafts, and pulling the straps the time they'd be slippy with going around beneath the heavens in rains falling. [IV. 47]

The priest, a decent unimaginative man, who likes
a drink, is afraid of his bishop, and finds it possible to
sympathise with Sarah Casey's passionate pleas while
being horrified at the ignorance and irreligion of the
old woman, is not an unsympathetic figure, though
Synge's critics regarded him as a caricature. He is
merely, like the priest in *Riders to the Sea*, out of his
depth. He cannot understand the passion that can result
equally in the desire for church-blessed respectability
and in theft, drink, and the threatening of the clergy.
He has no appreciation of the earth's moods, or of the
real innocence of Sarah Casey's heart.

It is Sarah Casey who dominates the play and is the
main vehicle of Synge's message. By means of her he
shows what happens when travelling people with their
own pagan traditions come up against the superficial
attractions of conventional property-owning society. By
means of her he suggests that the formulae of convention cannot cope with the emotional disturbances of
those who are in tune with the moods and rhythms of
the natural world. It is noticeable in the play that the
heroic language emanates wholly from the tinkers, and
that, however violent, coarse, abusive, devious, and
amoral they may be, their way of life contains a vigor
and self-confident alertness that is wholly admirable.

Synge's most rollicking comedy is, however, something more than a slap at dull respectability. It is the
third play in what he at least at one time regarded as a
sequence. In the first of the three, *Riders to the Sea*,
he showed a society isolated by natural forces from the
rest of the world. In the second play he showed an
equally isolated household in a desolate glen, and in-

dicated how conventional morality must break under the pressure of life's yearning after fulfillment. In the third play he gives us travelling people, not isolated from the "big world" but alien to it by reason of their way of life and their traditions and their love of a pagan poetic lore at variance with the lore of the church; and he reveals the violence that inevitably must result when uncomprehending conventionality is faced with the irrational demands of the imagination, and with the uninhibited passions of those to whom conventional society is no more than an occasionally amusing or delightful spectacle.

The tinkers of Synge's plays are, in contemporary jargon, dropouts. They do not seek violence though they do not exactly object to it. They seek from society a spiritual nourishment which society must inevitably refuse to grant on the grounds that they have cut themselves off from it. Abandoned by the church, they can only, in their wild simplicity, mock and attack it. Unable to understand or take seriously any property-owning world, they regard money as a game and theft as natural. Their values are primitive but fundamental. Stories of heroic times are important to them, though Mary Byrne complains:

> "What good am I this night, God help me? What good are the grand stories I have when it's few would listen to an old woman, few but a girl maybe would be in great fear the time her hour was come, or a little child wouldn't be sleeping with the hunger on a cold night?" [IV 27]

She is of the older generation, and Sarah of the younger. She has no truck with the big world beyond her own.

Sarah, on the other hand, attempts to come to terms with it, in her own passionate fashion, as primitive societies must always attempt to come to terms with the superior societies that conquer or dominate them and make the laws by which they are supposed to live.

In *The Tinker's Wedding* Synge was, as always, preaching a sermon. He was not merely indulging himself in a rollicking farce about fat priests and immoral tinkers. He was continuing his personal exploration of themes that were of deep personal importance to him, and yet again asking how the materialist and conventional society of his time could be made to understand the wildnesses and simplicities of the human heart, and accusing it both of stupidity and superficiality.

V

Undeterred by accusations that the plot of *In the Shadow of the Glen* had been taken from non-Irish sources, Synge took the hint for *The Well of the Saints* from the fifteenth-century farce *Moralité de l'aveugle et du boiteaux* by Andrieu de la Vigne, which he had come across during his studies at the Sorbonne. The farce tells how a blind man agrees to carry a cripple on his back so that between them they may have a full complement of faculties. When both are miraculously cured the blind man is overjoyed but the cripple is infuriated at being deprived of his easy life.

Synge's own play is equally simple in story. The two old blind beggars, Martin and Mary Doul, are able to live happily in a world of fantasy, believing themselves to be physically beautiful and attractive. Cured of their blindness by the Saint, they are disillusioned and accuse each other of ugliness and deceit. Martin falls in love with a pretty girl who mocks and rejects him, and he becomes weary of the world of labor which blindness can no longer enable him to avoid. When the cure proves temporary both beggars are delighted and again build up a fantasy about their personal beauty. This happiness is threatened by the Saint's offering them a second and permanent cure, and they choose first to hide from him, and then to spill the holy water, preferring the happy fantasies of their dream world to the ugly reality to which the Saint would have them return.

The plot itself might suggest condemnation of the beggars for their self-indulgent folly and escapism. Synge, however, steers his play in such a way that the beggars become figures of heroic pathos rather than contemptible dreamers. This is achieved partly by the way in which the Douls' passionate and simple poetry is contrasted with the brutal humor of the seeing characters. In the third act, once again blind, Martin Doul replies to the Saint's praise of the beauties of the visible world by saying:

> "Isn't it finer sights ourselves had a while since and we sitting dark smelling the sweet beautiful smells do be rising in the warm nights and hearing the swift flying things racing in the air, till we'd be looking up in our own minds into a grand sky, and seeing lakes, and broadening rivers, and hills are waiting for the spade and plough."
> [III. 141]

The onlookers mock him with coarse laughter, and call him both "mad" and "lazy." However, as Synge implies, he is as much a spiritual man as the saint himself. When the cure is first effected and the Douls are appalled at the reality of ugliness that they encounter in each other, the saint tells them:

> "May the Lord who has given you sight send a little sense into your heads, the way it won't be on your two selves you'll be looking—on two pitiful sinners of the earth—

but on the splendour of the Spirit of God, you'll see an odd time shining out through the big hills, and steep streams falling to the sea. For if it's on the like of that you do be thinking, you'll not be minding the faces of men, but you'll be saying prayers and great praises, till you'll be living the way the great saints do be living, with little but old sacks, and skin covering their bones. . . ." [III 101]

This is ironic for the Douls, in their blindness, have indeed been looking on the inward splendors of human dreams, and imagining ideal beauty, although themselves ragged and starving. Now able to see, they find themselves obsessed with the faces of humanity. Timmy tells them

"But it's a queer thing the way yourself and Mary Doul are after setting every person in this place, and up beyond to Rathvanna, talking of nothing, and thinking of nothing, but the way they do be looking in the face. It's the devil's work you're after doing with your talk of fine looks. . . ." [III 111]

Martin Doul is appalled by the ugliness he finds, but in the young girl Molly he sees a beauty that almost matches his idea.

". . . but there's one fine thing we have, to be looking on a grand, white, handsome girl, the like of you . . . and every time I set my eyes on you, I do be blessing the saints, and the holy water, and the power of the Lord Almighty in the heavens above." [III. 111]

Molly however rejects his love. The beauty of the actual is as much or more of a delusion than the beauty of his dreams. As darkness again descends on him he cries, cursing Molly and Timmy the Smith, whom she is to marry:

"And that's the last thing I'm to set my sight on in the life of the world, the villainy of a woman and the bloody strength of a man. . . ." [III. 123]

Rejecting the "big world" of the visible, the Douls are confused about moral values. Having again convinced themselves of their own beauty, he vain of the long silky white beard he will have as an old man and she proud of her wonderful white hair, they regard a permanent cure of their blindness as an act which will precipitate them into a world of lies, deceit, and ugliness. Threatened by this cure Mary cries out, on hearing the bell of the Saint approaching them, "The Lord protect us from the Saints of God!" and warns Martin not to say anything wicked in case the cure should be wrought upon them.

MARY DOUL: Let you not be whispering sin, Martin Doul, or maybe it's the finger of God they'd see pointing to ourselves.

MARTIN DOUL: It's yourself is speaking madness, Mary Doul, haven't you heard the saint say it's the wicked do be blind?

MARY DOUL: If it is you'd have a right to speak a big terrible word would make the water not cure us at all.

MARTIN DOUL: What way would I find a big terrible word, and I shook with the fear, and if I did itself, who'd know rightly if it's good words or bad would save us this day from himself? [III. 135]

In this way Synge points to the dangers inherent in reforms contrived by those who do not understand the society whose ills they are attempting to ameliorate. The Saint, believing in dedication to things of the spirit, does not recognize that in curing the Douls he is depriving them of their vision of God's goodness. Secure in his belief that physical sight must bring spiritual awakening, he is as much dominated by irrational fantasy as the Douls themselves, and when he blesses the marriage of Molly and Timmy, he is as ignorant of the true nature of the girl as was Martin Doul when he was blind. Nor does he realize that the Douls, when blind beggars, proved the occasion for much charity and kindness, whereas when seeing they became themselves discontented, and the source of aggravation in others, for Martin was required to work like other men, and was blamed for his failures, whereas previously he was accepted as a unique individual with his own way of life. Martin Doul at the end of the play, having spilt the miracle-working water, faces the dangers of wandering into unknown country with courage.

Turned away by all the people he has made his decision to face physical rather than spiritual danger. He tells the crowd:

> "We're going surely, for if it's a right some of you have to be working and sweating the like of Timmy the smith, and a right some of you have to be fasting and praying and talking holy talk the like of yourself, I'm thinking it's a good right ourselves have to be sitting blind, hearing a soft wind turning round the little leaves of the spring and feeling the sun, and we not tormenting our souls with the sight of the grey days, and the holy men, and the dirty feet is trampling the world." [III 149]

In the challenging and lyrical poetry of this speech, Martin Doul is spokesman for Synge's passionate rejection of the constricting uniformity of orthodox social attitudes. He is claiming liberty of action for the individual man, and opposing any authority, ecclesiastic or political, that attempts to tell men how they should spend their lives. He is claiming the right to live according to his individual conscience, and to retain his own personal vision no matter how foolish or delusory it may appear to others. Moreover, the speech (like the whole play) suggests that one must not equate orthodoxy with morality or authority with wisdom. *The Well of the Saints* is another of Synge's attacks upon conventional thought, and another paean in praise of the passionate and courageous rebel against the shibboleths of the "big world."

The Well of the Saints was much abused on its first performance. *The Freemans Journal* said "the point of view is not that of a writer in sympathetic touch with the people from whom he purports to draw his characters"; there were also objections to the crudity and vulgarity of the language. The critics would have been even angrier had they perceived that the play, in fact, was calling all orthodoxies—political, religious, and national—into question, and that if its message were to be applied to Irish politics, it would have to be interpreted as saying that the right of dissent was paramount, and the apolitical should be permitted to remain outside the Nationalist movement. *The Well of the Saints* is not one of Synge's greatest plays, but in it he stated more clearly and unequivocally than anywhere else his passionate rejection of all constricting orthodoxies and his belief in the importance of individual sensibility and the individual conscience.

VI

Three months after the first production of *The Well of the Saints*, Synge visited West Mayo and Connemara with Jack B. Yeats. He was to write a series of articles on these distressed areas for the *Manchester Guardian* and Jack Yeats was to illustrate them. These articles differ from Synge's other essays, which resemble *The Aran Islands* in their attempt to portray less the realities of fact than the disturbances of the writer's sympathetic imagination. They are written levelly, coolly, and only occasionally do they indulge in those musing reflections which give the other works their poetic character. Synge felt them to be inadequate and was uncertain about republishing them in book form. He felt, too, that he had only written about a part of the life that he had seen and (in a letter of July 13, 1905) told Stephen MacKenna:

There are sides of all that western life, the groggy—patriot—publican—general—shop-man who is married to the priest's half-sister and is second cousin once removed of the dispensary doctor, that are horrible and awful. This is the type that is running the present United Irish League anti-grazier campaign, while they're swindling the people them-

selves in a dozen ways and then buying out their holdings
and packing off whole families to America. The subject is
too big to go into here, but at best it's beastly. All that
side of the matter of course I left untouched in my stuff.
I sometimes wish to God I hadn't a soul and then I could
give myself up to putting those lads on the stage. God,
wouldn't they hop!

Though these essays are not calculated to make anyone
"hop," they do reveal Synge's approach to the efforts
of the Congested Districts Board to alleviate the miseries
of the Western Peasant. He found that "The relief
system, as it is now carried on, is an utterly degrading
one," and contrasted the "grotesquely" dressed shopkeepers with the "patched and threadbare and ragged"
poor. He found one of the rebuilt cottages which
"seemed natural and local" and commented "That, at
least was reassuring." In general, however, though he
made a number of practical recommendations concern-
ing the need for better communications and objected
to the greed of the small shopkeepers, he was concerned
with the more vague possibility of restoring "some
national life to the people." He saw that the culture of
the West was being destroyed both by emigration and
by misplaced attempts at reformation, and spoke up
firmly for Home Rule as a means of ensuring moral as
well as economic regeneration.

His experience in the West embittered him. He was
already working on plans for *The Playboy of the Western World,* and on his return from the West settled
down to it in earnest. In early 1906 he fell in love with
Molly Allgood, a young actress whom he had first seen
in a walking-on part in *The Well of the Saints,* and he
decided that the heroine of his play was to be created

for her. It seems not unlikely that the political implications of his new play owed something to his visit
to the Congested Districts, just as it is certain that the
character of Pegeen Mike owes a good deal to that of
Molly Allgood, and the language of the play derives
from notes made of the lively and picturesque speech
of West Kerry where he was now spending some part
of each summer.

The Playboy of the Western World surpassed both
In the Shadow of the Glen and The Well of the Saints
in its arousal of furious opposition. There were riots on
the first night, and on succeeding nights, and the police
had to be called in to protect the players and enable the
drama to be performed at all. Once again it was said
that Synge was libelling the Irish character and Irish
womanhood in particular, and once again few of the
audience noticed that the play was much more seriously
and profoundly challenging in terms of its themes than
it was upsetting because of its vigorous vulgarity and
superficially blasphemous language, or even the savage
mockery of its plot.

As with In the Shadow of the Glen, The Tinker's
Wedding, and The Well of the Saints, Synge chose for
The Playboy of the Western World a story that at first
blush seems proper only for treatment as farce. The
story of the young man who is welcomed as a hero by
the Mayo peasants because he is believed to have killed
his father with the blow of a spade, and, on the reap-
pearance of the dead man, ridiculed as an imposter, is
similar to many folk tales of many lands. Synge chose
to complicate it somewhat by making two women rivals
for his playboy's affections, and by arranging for the

father to be again "killed" in the sight of the peasants, who are then outraged by the reality that they had previously admired in their imaginations. He also chose to imitate the stories he had heard in Aran by filling his play with echoes of other stories. He himself, in commenting on the play in a letter, referred to *Don Quixote* as being similarly extravagant, and, in a note to the press, to *The Merchant of Venice* and *Alceste* as being similarly poised between comedy and seriousness. It is easy to see that Christy Mahon is similar to Don Quixote in transforming commonplace actuality by means of his imagination, and in involving others in his poetic version of the world. In *The Merchant of Venice* the bargain of the pound of flesh is accepted largely as a joke until it becomes actuality, just as Christy Mahon's act of murder is regarded as heroic until it is repeated in full view of the peasants. Alceste, who, when her husband was about to die, offered her life for his, and was eventually brought back from Hades by Hercules, is a less obvious parallel, though Pegeen Mike in hiding Christy from the police and in wishing to devote her life to him does perform a slightly similar role. Synge was not, however, concerned to echo these earlier stories directly: he was interested in reflecting them in a slightly distorted manner, and, in his comments, suggesting to those that had the intelligence to take the hint that the play develops thematic richness from the use of allusion and parody. It is notable, however, that while hinting at this general characteristic of the play, he did not think it wise to refer to the most powerful allusions of all, those to the life of Jesus Christ.

The play forces us to admit the presence of these

allusions by its continual use of religious epithets and
phrases. These are used with rich incongruity and in-
appropriateness by all the characters but the Widow
Quinn. The first hint that this is intended to do more
than indicate the confusion of religion with superstition
in the mind of the Mayo peasant comes when Shawn
Keogh reports to Pegeen Mike that he has heard a fellow
"above in the furzy ditch . . . groaning out and breaking
his heart" but was afraid to go and see what ailed him.
Shawn being excessively god-fearing and blatantly
pious, this must remind us of the parable of the Good
Samaritan, especially as shortly after this disclosure is
made and Pegeen promises to tell no one of Shawn's
encounter, the men enter the public house saying "God
Bless you. The blessing of God on this place." When
Christy Mahon does arrive and tells his story the village
girls bring him gifts, thus parodying the Epiphany, and
tell him "Well you're a marvel! Oh, God bless you!
You're the lad surely!" When Christy rides to triumph
in the sports and then comes back into the inn his glory
is short-lived, for Old Mahon turns up and identifies
himself. The dialogue that follows has strong biblical
echoes, with its reference to the "sins of the whole
world" and to "Almighty God"; and Pegeen herself
echoes Pontius Pilate when she tells Old Mahon,

> Take him on from this, for I think bad the world should
> see me raging for a Munster liar and the fool of men.
> MAHON: Rise up now to retribution, and come on with
>   me.
> CROWD: (*jeeringly*) There's the playboy! There's the lad
>   thought he'd rule the roost in Mayo. Slate him
>   now, Mister.
> CHRISTY: (*getting up in shy terror*) What is it drives you

to torment me here, when I'd ask the thunders of
the might of God to blast me if I ever did hurt
to any saving only that one single blow.

MAHON: *(loudly)* If you didn't, you're a poor good-for-
nothing, and isn't it by the like of you the sins
of the whole world are committed?

CHRISTY: *(raising his hands)* in the name of the Almighty
God. . . . [IV. 161]

The binding and wounding of Christy after he has
"killed" his father a second time echoes the binding
and wounding of Christ, and Christy's last speech, in
its assertion of his immortality and the good his "cruci-
fixion" has done, is also a near-parody of Christ's claims
after his resurrection:

Ten thousand blessings upon all that's here, for you've
turned me a likely gaffer in the end of all, the way I'll go
romancing through a romping lifetime from this hour to
the dawning of the judgement day. [IV. 173]

If this parallelism is accepted, it must be realized
that the drama has political as well as moral overtones
of considerable seriousness. Christy's killing of his
father must be seen in the context of Shawn Keogh's
constant awed references to Authority in the form of
Father Reilly and the Holy Father in Rome. Christy
has rebelled against Authority, and as long as the rebellion is purely verbal, a "gallous story," it arouses the
appreciation of the Irish: when, however, it becomes an
actual rebellion, support for it falls away. It is the story
of many Irish rebellions, including that of 1916 which
Synge did not live long enough to see. It is the story of
Parnell who remained the "Chief" as long as he did not

too obviously offend against puritannical morality; when he was accused of adultery he was abandoned and Ireland's greatest hope of freedom was destroyed. Words are, to Synge's Irishmen, more important than facts: it is the fine poetic speech of Christy that makes him a hero, and not the actuality upon which the poetry is based. Here, as in Synge's earlier comedies, the central figure is the vehicle of a poetic vision that transfigures the commonplace and makes the mundane narrowness of country life bearable. Whereas in *In the Shadow of the Glen, The Tinker's Wedding,* and *The Well of the Saints,* this poetic vision is regarded as being a sign of spiritual health, in *The Playboy of the Western World* we are shown that poetic sensibility and moral integrity need not necessarily go together.

The Playboy of the Western World differs from the earlier plays in other respects also. In those earlier plays, even including *Riders to the Sea,* the central figure is not aware of his or her heroic stature. The pathos of the Douls is intensified by their laying claim to lesser dignities than they in fact possess by being so committed to the life of the inward vision and so resolutely opposed to the big world of materialism. Sarah Casey does not understand the nature of the battle she herself wages. Norah Burke is unaware that her rebellion raises a standard of general importance, and Maurya does not see herself as representative of all bereaved motherhood. Christy Mahon, however, at first deluded into believing himself a hero, becomes a hero because he is given the opportunity to play the role, and, after his downfall, understands not only his own

personal strength, but also its symbolic importance, as
Pegeen Mike herself recognizes it when she cries out
in desperation,

> "Oh my grief, I've lost him surely. I've lost the only
> playboy of the western world." [IV. 173]

Christy is a hero to Mayo, however, not simply because of his poetry, but because he symbolizes in his
murderous act the peasant's attitude towards moral and
political authority. When he first hints of his crime,
Jimmy thinks he may be in trouble for having followed
"a young woman on a lonesome night," and Philly
suggests that "maybe the land was grabbed from him
and he did what any decent man would do," or perhaps
that he was on the run because he had fought against
the English in the Boer War and was now liable to be
"judged to be hanged, quartered and drawn." All are
sure that the police would be afraid to arrest him. The
girls also show the Mayo approach to legality when they
tell Christy and the Widow Quinn (who is popularly
supposed to have murdered her husband):

> "You're heroes surely, and let you drink a supeen with
> your arms linked like the outlandish lovers in the sailor's
> song. There now. Drink a health to the wonders of the
> western world, the pirates, preachers, poteen-makers, with
> the jobbing jockies, parching peelers, and the juries fill
> their stomachs selling judgements of the English law." [IV.
> 105]

This speech reveals the Mayomen's love of roguery and
their cynical unbelief in the lawmakers and processes
of law. Michael, in spite of Shawn Keogh's wealth, pre-
fers Christy as a husband for his daughter, for he thinks

it better to breed "little gallant swearers" than "puny weeds."

Shawn Keogh serves to show the materialism and greed of the peasants by attempting to bribe the Widow Quinn to marry Christy, and he also indicates his own cowardice and treachery by admitting:

> "I'd inform again him, but he'd burst from Kilmainham and he'd be sure and certain to destroy me. If I wasn't so Godfearing, I'd near have courage to come behind him and run a pike into his side." [IV 117]

The portrait of the Mayo peasants that Synge presents is, one may surely now admit, quite as savage as his earliest critics felt. Though he enjoys the vigor of their speech, their wildness, their simplicity, he exposes their moral weakness, their hypocrisy, and their greed also. He does however in Pegeen Mike create yet another heroine animated by a passionate desire to escape from the constrictions of her way of life, and fully committed to her vision. She fights wholeheartedly for her man, accepting him totally, and when she discovers the truth she attacks him with equal wholeheartedness, leading in the binding of him, and herself burning him with the fire. She is herself heroic in the extremity of her feelings, and in the savagery of her pride. Desperation stirs in her: she is forced by emotional necessity to grab every chance of escape from the world of Mayo. Intemperate in speech, vital in action, she is capable of that kind of violence to which Christy lays claim, and so she recognizes something of herself in him, and when forced by pride to reject him, she realizes that she has thrown away part of herself.

The Widow Quinn, on the other hand, is almost exactly an opposite to Pegeen. A spectator of the action, she is delighted to connive at Christy's deceit and send Old Mahon on a fool's errand. Blandly amoral, she is the wise and cynical woman of the play, reminding one of Mary Byrne in her understanding of the ways of the human heart. Oddly enough, she is the only character who does not take the name of God in vain at every available opportunity: she finds this pseudo-religious verbiage amusing. When Christy appeals to her to help him win Pegeen her retort is coolly mocking.

CHRISTY: . . . Aid me for to win her, and I'll be
                asking God to stretch a hand to you in
                the hour of death, and lead you short
                cuts through the Meadows of Ease, and
                up the floor of Heaven to the Footstool
                of the Virgin's Son.
WIDOW QUINN: There's praying! [IV 127 & 131]

The widow Quinn, however, is unlike Mary Byrne in that her vision of the world, because cynical, fails to appreciate the real importance of all the high-sounding words. She does not understand that the man accepted as hero becomes hero; she does not appreciate that the religious imprecations and the glorification of violence both arise from a desperate need to give life significance and dignity; she cannot share in either the pathos or the glory, and is unable to see why Christy is in love with Pegeen Mike for, she tells him, "Come I'll find you finer sweethearts at each waning moon," and thinks him fit for the madhouse rather than the gaol when he insists that he must marry Pegeen.

It was the stark harshness of Pegeen Mike at the close of the play which disturbed George Moore and other critics, and yet it is completely in character and, of course, essential to the theme of rejection which Synge was again concerned to present.

The theme of rejection in *The Playboy of the Western World* is handled more comprehensively than elsewhere in his work. The second killing of Old Mahon is especially significant, for it is this actual attack against authority which causes him to be rejected by those very people who have, it seems, a profound need themselves to reject the authorities set over them, and who talk continually of the heroic rebels amongst them. In this Christy himself parallels Synge's own rebellions and betrayals: *In the Shadow of the Glen* was condemned by those very people who were most concerned to bring Ireland freedom, dignity, and a proper understanding of her predicament; *The Well of the Saints* was condemned by critics who were themselves busy raising a standard of revolt against the authority of the establishment. The harshness of Synge's play is, possibly, to some extent due to his own sense that he himself, as a man whose every work was written at least partly in a desire to assist the regeneration of his country, had been condemned by those very people who shared his patriotism and should logically have applauded his endeavors.

In commenting upon Synge's drama in his essay, *J. M. Synge and the Ireland of his Time,* W. B. Yeats told how he explained to Synge that he preferred *The Shadow of the Glen* to *Riders to the Sea,* because the latter was "too passive in suffering." He wrote:

Synge answered: "It is a curious thing that *Riders to the Sea* succeeds with an English but not with an Irish audience, and *The Shadow of the Glen,* which is not liked by an English audience, is always liked in Ireland, though it is disliked there in theory." Since then *Riders to the Sea* has grown into great popularity in Dublin, partly because with the tactical instinct of an Irish mob, the demonstrators against *The Playboy* both in the Press and in the theatre, where it began the evening, selected it for applause. It is now what Shelley's *Cloud* was for many years, a comfort to those who do not like to deny altogether the genius they cannot understand. Yet I am certain that, in the long run, his grotesque plays with their lyric beauty, their violent laughter, *The Playboy of the Western World* most of all, will be loved for holding so much of the mind of Ireland. . . . It is the strangest, the most beautiful expression in drama of that Irish fantasy which overflowing through all Irish literature that has come out of Ireland itself (compare the fantastic Irish account of the Battle of Clontarf with the sober Norse account) is the unbroken character of Irish genius.

Whether or not one accepts Yeats's view of the nature of "Irish genius," this prophesy of 1910 as regards the coming popularity of *The Playboy* has been amply fulfilled. Yeats's comments, however, also suggest in what way *The Playboy* differs from the earlier works. It contains more of "the mind of Ireland." Whereas, in the short plays Synge had only space to imply the complexity of his characters and suggest the most basic of their emotional problems, in *The Playboy of the Western World* he was able to make the gradual uncovering of the paradoxes and confusions of his main characters an integral part of the movement of the play. Instead of repeating key images, he elaborated and developed them. Thus, the hypocrisy of Shaun Keogh is not so static a component of the play as is the simple sincerity

of the Saint in *Well of the Saints,* or the timorous
cupidity of the young man in *The Shadow of the Glen;*
it develops and intensifies until it achieves the out-
rageous grotesquerie of the last act. Similarly, the
conflicts of interests in the earlier drama are easily
identifiable: desire opposes desire in straightforward
confrontation. In *The Playboy of The Western World,*
however, the motives of the Widow Quinn, of Pegeen
Mike, and of Christy Mahon himself are less simple to
define. The Widow Quinn, in particular, appears to be
moved as much by her relish for the farcical and ironic
as by her sexual greed, and there is an element of Nar-
cissism in both Pegeen Mike and Christy Mahon which
qualifies and to some extent vitiates the urgency of
their more outward-looking desires.

The Playboy of the Western World is not merely
more complex in characterization than the earlier
drama; it is organized dramatically in terms of the
changing nature of personal beliefs, desires, and com-
mitments in a situation calculated to provoke such
change. It is the last of a series of plays each of which
concerned itself more with the uncovering of dramatic
conflicts within the individual characters than did its
predecessor. Thus the "lyric beauty" and "violent
laughter" of which Yeats speaks are products not of
different kinds of events but of the presence in each
individual of elements of glory and absurdity which the
events uncover. This distinction is most obvious when
we see how Christy Mahon can wax lyrical over matters
we ourselves might think trivial or even gross, and how
the intensity of his feelings betrays him into absurdity
on occasions which are not in themselves absurd. It was

Synge's realization that the wellspring of his drama was to be found more in character than event that enabled him to make of an anecdote scarcely more substantial than those he had used for *Riders to the Sea* and *In the Shadow of the Glen,* a full-length drama which remains one of the greatest comedies of the world. He did it by seeking, Yeats wrote, "not through the eyes or in history, or even in the future, but . . . in the depths of the mind."

VII

Synge's own personal experience was as much central to his mature plays as it was to his earliest works, and it was at the very heart of all his poetry. While working on *The Playboy of the Western World* he had begun again to make poems, and to experiment with translations. He revised many of the poems earlier included in *Vita Vecchia,* toughening their language and clarifying their forms. He also turned his hand to poems that should counter the over-romantic and sentimental poetry of Irish poets of the time with something more powerful. Thus, after looking at one of AE's pictures, he wrote in 1907

> Adieu, sweet Angus, Maeve and Fand,
> Ye plumed yet skinny Shee,
> That poets played with hand in hand
> To learn their ecstasy.
>
> We'll search in Red Dan Sally's ditch,
> And drink in Tubber fair,
> Or poach with Red Dan Philly's bitch
> The badger and the hare. [I. 38]

An earlier and fragmentary version of this poem ended
with a reference to his dislike of the "patriot, rhyming
reems (sic) of bloody rot." Other poems of this time
are equally opposed to romantic sentimentalizing of
rural pleasures, or rural tragedy. *Patch Shaneen* de-
scribes in the most direct language the death of a
peasant's wife and his consequent poverty and grief.
Beg Innish rumbustiously celebrates a party in Kerry,
and *Danny* tells brutally and frankly of a murder in
Connaught.

The love poems are just as unsentimental as the
others, and as physically explicit. The language of *In
May* is notably devoid of references to romantic sigh-
ings, and is erotic rather than romantic.

> In a nook
> That opened south,
> You and I
> Lay mouth to mouth.
>
> A snowy gull
> And sooty daw
> Came and looked
> With many a caw;
>
> 'Such,' I said,
> 'Are I and you,
> When you've kissed me
> Black and blue!'
>   [I. 53]

This is revolutionary not only in its explicitness but in

the active role it gives the girl in the case. *A Wish* is similarly unorthodox in its suggesting that the lover may be stimulated by his mistresses' tears, and the sexual imagery of the roses and the phallic maypole is handled with a directness and dramatic brevity that are astonishing for the year 1907.

> May seven tears in every week
> Touch the hollow of your cheek,
> That I—signed with such a dew—
> For a lion's share may sue
> Of the roses ever curled
> Round the May-pole of the world.
>
> Heavy riddles lie in this,
> Sorrow's sauce for every kiss.
>
> [I. 51]

The earlier version which Synge sent Molly in a letter of 26 March 1907 was even more candid, containing the two lines

> May seven tears in every week
> From your well of pleasure leak. . . .

It is important to register that Synge, in his poetry as in his plays, was challenging the conventions and preferring passion to sentiment and candor to literary contrivance.

When, in 1908 he began to think about publishing his poems he wrote Yeats in a letter of September, 1908:

. . . if verse, even great verse is to be alive it must be occupied with the whole of life—as it was with Villon and Shakespeare's songs, and with Herrick and Burns. For although exalted verse is the highest, it cannot keep its power unless there is more essentially vital verse at the side of it as ecclesiastical architecture cannot remain fine, when domestic architecture is debased. [I xv]

He said in the same letter that humor was "the essentially poetic quality in what I call vital verse." In the Preface to his book of poems, he wrote:

In these days poetry is usually a flower of evil or good, but it is the timber of poetry that wears most surely, and there is no timber that has not strong roots among the clay and worms. Even if we grant that exalted poetry can be kept successful by itself, the strong things of life are needed in poetry also, to show that what is exalted, or tender, is not made by feeble blood. It may almost be said that before verse can be human again it must learn to be brutal. [I. xxxvi]

The word "brutal" has been taken as referring to such violent and savage poems as *Danny* and *The Mergency Man,* but it surely also applies to those poems in which Synge juxtaposed vividly colloquial with literary language, and placed images of death alongside images of human passion, and romantic cadences alongside vulgar ones. Thus the poem *Queens* gives us a catalogue of a kind familiar in heroic and romantic poetry, but humanizes it with humor, and enlivens it by juxtaposing such antique words as "coifed" with such down-to-earth ones as "wormy," and including references to fleas and vermin as well as to the great names of romance.

Seven dog-days we let pass
Naming Queens in Glenmacnass,
All the rare and royal names
Wormy sheepskin yet retains,
Etain, Helen, Maeve, and Fand,
Golden Deirdre's tender hand,
Bert, the big-foot, sung by Villon,
Cassandra, Ronsard found in Lyon.
Queens of Sheba, Meath and Connaught,
Coifed with crown, or gaudy bonnet,
Queens whose finger once did stir men,
Queens were eaten of fleas and vermin,
Queens men drew like Monna Lisa,
Or slew with drugs in Rome and Pisa,
We named Lucrezia Crivelli,
And Titian's lady with amber belly,
Queens acquainted in learned sin,
Jane of Jewry's slender shin:
Queens who cut the bogs of Glanna,
Judith of Scripture and Gloriana,
Queens who wasted the East by proxy,
Or drove the ass-cart, a tinker's doxy,
Yet these are rotten—I ask their pardon—
And we've the sun on rock and garden,
These are rotten, so you're the Queen
Of all are living, or have been.

[I. 34]

The gaiety of this poem is typical, and gaiety remained
an element of Synge's poems right to his death. Even
when contemplating his own death he could wrily
mock his situation.

I've thirty months, and that's my pride,
Before my age's a double score,
Though many lively men have died
At twenty-nine or little more.
I've left a long and famous set
Behind some seven years or three,
But there are millions I'd forget
Will have their laugh at passing me.

[I. 59]

Synge's poems express his challenges, and are often filled with the vitality of his love for Molly. At the same period that he was writing these, however, he was experimenting with making prose-poem translations from the work of others. These translations were, however, just as personal to him as his own poems. He expressed something of his sympathy for his mother in her old age with two translations from Villon; he commented upon his own poverty as an author in one from Colin Musset, and he expressed aspects of his love for Molly in versions of Leopardi, Walter von der Vogelweide, and Petrarch. The Walter von der Vogelweide translation he made as a direct rebuke to Molly for her tendency to mock his complaints and her enjoyment of the company of others.

I never set my two eyes on a head was so fine as your head, but I'd no way to be looking down into your heart.

It's for that I was tricked out and out—that was the thanks I got for being so steady in my love.

I tell you, if I could have laid my hands on the

whole set of the stars, the moon and the sun along
with it, by Christ I'd have given the lot to her.
No place have I set eyes on the like of her, she's
bad to her friends, and gay and playful to those
she'd have a right to hate. I ask you can that
behaviour have a good end come to it? [I 84]

The Petrarch translations were less forceful, and clearly
were intended partly as a study of the possibilities of
poetic drama in prose, for Synge was now planning
Deirdre of the Sorrows, which he intended to be very
different in style from all his other work. He contrived
to create a prose form which accurately reflects the
shape of the sonnet by means of carefully balanced
paragraphs, and in which many of the phrases are ex-
tremely rhythmical without being metrical. The poems
themselves also carry a great deal of his own emotional
situation.

Life is flying from me, not stopping an hour, and
Death is making great strides following my track.
The days about me, and the days passed over me
are bringing me desolation, and the days to come
will be the same surely. [I. 86]

Musical, and melancholy, and only occasionally given
strength by that "brutal" element Synge thought important for poetry, these prose-poems are not among
Synge's greatest works, though they were for him a
necessary step towards his last play in which he uses the
cadenced prose he learned from his translations, and in
which he also uses the same pervasive melancholy.

VIII

Synge never completed *Deirdre of the Sorrows*. He began it as a vehicle for Molly Allgood to star in, and he worked on it as long as he had the strength to work at all. When finally he had to give up writing he was trying to give it more strength by increasing the grotesque element in it, for he recognized that as it stood the play was somewhat static. He had intended "stateliness," but he had achieved it at the expense of vitality.

He had made his task difficult by permitting Deirdre to believe the truth of the prophesy about herself from the very beginning. Thus she never has any doubts of her role or of the ultimate destruction of the Sons of Usna because of her rejecting the king, Conchubar, for the love of Naisi. This means that the character at the very center of the play cannot be the means of presenting the dramatic tensions of uncertainty, indecisiveness, or bewilderment. Deirdre indeed dominates the play from the beginning. When Naisi discovers that the country girl after whom he lusts is that Deirdre who is prophesied to be his downfall, his ardor is cooled. She tells him

". . . it's a sweet life you and I could have Naisi . . .
It should be a sweet thing to have what is best and richest
if it's for a short space only." [IV. 209]

He is understandably nervous and suggests that it
might be better to conduct their love affair on the sly
rather than elope.

"Wouldn't we do well to wait, Deirdre, and I each twilight meeting you on the side of the hills?" [IV. 211]

Deirdre, however, is being pressured by Conchubar to
go to his court and knows there is no time left for cau-
tion. With ruthless idealism she insists upon Naisi be-
coming her lover.

"You must not go Naisi, and leave me to the High King,
a man is ageing in his Dun, with his crowds round him
and his silver and gold. I will not live to be shut up in
Emain, and wouldn't we do well paying, Naisi, with
silence, and a near death? I'm a long while in the woods
with my own self, and I'm in little dread of death, and
it earned with richness would make the sun red with envy
and he going up the heavens, and the moon pale and
lonesome and she wasting away. Isn't it a small thing is
foretold about the ruin of ourselves, Naisi, when all men
have age coming and great ruin in the end?" [IV. 211]

This passionate plea for life's "richness" must remind
us of the similar desires of Nora Burke, Sarah Casey,
and Pegeen Mike; but unlike the first of these Deirdre
is willing not merely to risk suffering as the consequence of freedom, but to accept it completely. Moreover she accepts that her lover himself will be destroyed,
her only worry being as to whether or not she can herself be happy knowing what is in store.

"And yet I'm in dread leaving this place where I have lived always. Won't I be lonesome and I thinking on the little hill beyond and the apple trees do be budding in the springtime by the post of the door? . . . Won't I be in great dread to bring you to destruction, Naisi, and you so happy and young?" [IV. 211]

The self-centeredness of Deirdre is an inevitable concomitant of her seeing herself as the heroine of a great story. She must be true to her destined role; this is, of course, another instance of Synge maintaining that, "The only truth we know is that we are a flood of magnificent life" and attempting to present that "cosmic element in the person which gives all personal art, and all sincere life, and all passionate love a share in the dignity of the world."

Unfortunately, we see very little of the glory of Deirdre and Naisi: the second act finds them on the point of deciding to return to Conchubar's court, aware that for all the promises of amnesty it must mean their death. The play from the second act onwards is dark with foreboding. The ideal happiness is spoiled by thoughts of inevitable doom. Deirdre tells Lavarcham, the old nurse,

"I've dread of going or staying, Lavarcham. It's lonesome this place having happiness like ours till I'm asking each day, will this day match yesterday, and will tomorrow take a good place beside the same day in the year that's gone, and wondering all times is it a game worth playing, living on until you're dried and old, and our joy is gone for ever." [IV. 219]

This speech reminds one of the end of *Axel* where the hero and heroine choose to commit suicide at the high-

est point of their happiness rather than permit it to
dwindle with the advancing years, and not all the
poetic rhetoric of Deirdre or her sense of the grandeur
of her tragedy can quite obliterate a feeling of the per-
versity of her attitude. Lavarcham and Owen both
bring some liveliness to the play by the occasional
vigor of their speeches, but in general, from the beginning of the second act until the end, we are made
to suffer wearisomely repetitious discussions of the situation made even more wearisome by the beautiful but
lulling cadences in which so many of the speeches are
presented. Naisi rejects the notion of returning and
says they should stay in Alban always. Deirdre tells him:

> "There's no place to stay always. . . . It's a long time
> we've had, pressing the lips together, going up and down,
> resting in our arms, Naisi, waking with the smell of June
> in the tops of the grasses, and listening to the birds in the
> branches that are highest. . . . It's a long time we've had,
> but the end has come surely." [IV. 231]

Later she tells Ainnle that old age is miserable and adds

> "It's a lonesome thing to be away from Ireland always."
> [IV. 237]

The denouement approaches with slow inevitability,
and is attended by much rhetoric. Deirdre sends Naisi
out to help his brothers battling Conchubar's men:

> "Go to your brothers. . . . For seven years you have been
> kindly, but the hardness of death has come between us."
> NAISI: (*looking at her aghast*) And you'll have me
>   meet death with a hard word from your lips in
>   my ear?
> DEIRDRE: We've had a dream, but this night has waked us

surely. In a little while we've lived too long,
Naisi, and isn't it a poor thing we should miss
the safety of the grave, and we trampling its
edge?

AINNLE: (*behind*) Naisi, Naisi, we are attacked and
ruined.

DEIRDRE: Let you go where they are calling! (*She looks
at him for an instant coldly*) Have you no
shame loitering and talking and a cruel death
facing Ainnle and Ardan in the woods? [IV. 255]

Her lament over the grave of Naisi is self-centered
though also pathetic.

"Who'll pity Deirdre has lost the lips of Naisi from her
neck, and from her cheek forever: who'll pity Deirdre has
lost the twilight in the woods with Naisi, when beech-
trees were silver and copper, and ash-trees were fine gold?"
[IV. 257]

She stops the conflict of Fergus and Conchubar with
the words:

"Draw a little back with the squabbling of fools when I
am broken up with misery. . . . I see the flames of Emain
starting upward in the dark night, and because of me
there will be weasels and wild cats crying on a lonely
wall where there were queens and armies, and red gold,
the way there will be a story told of a ruined city and
a raving king and a woman will be young forever. . . ."
[IV. 267]

In this speech she claims to have conquered mortality.
It is her answer to old Maurya's cry of resignation,

"No man at all can be living for ever, and we must be
satisfied." [III. 27]

It is also, of course, the claim made by artists for their

art. It is perhaps, even Synge's claim; and one must not forget that Synge, as he wrote *Deirdre of the Sorrows,* was himself aware of approaching death, and attempting to stake his claim to the attention of posterity with a poetic tragedy that should contain both some of the glory of Ireland's heroic past and some of his own grief at the brevity of his own joy in love.

At the end of his career, Synge in *Deirdre of the Sorrows,* transposed his personal situation into drama just as he had done in this first completed play, *When the Moon has Set;* and in both plays the contemplative, poetic, and philosophical elements outweigh and to some extent vitiate the dramatic ones. Of this he himself was clearly aware, and he left instructions for Yeats and Lady Gregory to add a passage of their own to the play in order to give it greater dramatic intensity and strength. They made the attempt, but, Yeats wrote in his preface to the first edition of the play,

> . . . we were little satisfied and thought it better to have the play performed, as it is printed here, with no word of ours. [IV. 179]

Synge, said Yeats,

> did not speak to me of any other alteration, but it is probable that he would have altered till the structure had become as strong and varied as in his other plays; and had he lived to do that, 'Deirdre of the Sorrows' would have been his masterwork, so much beauty is there in its course, and such wild nobleness at its end, and so poignant is an emotion and wisdom that were his own preparation for death. [IV. 179]

Though Synge ended his life's work with an imperfect play, he also ended it with yet another presentation of themes of rejection. Deirdre, like others of Synge's protagonists, rejects the world of convention in order to find spiritual and emotional richness and freedom. The play can be regarded as glorifying adultery and unorthodoxy to a greater degree than did *In the Shadow of the Glen.* It is as firmly anti-materialist as *The Well of the Saints,* and as concerned with celebrating the movements of a heart in harmony with the moods of the earth as is *The Tinker's Wedding.* It was not, however, like those earlier plays, condemned for its attitudes; dignified by its subject matter and its legendary content, and obscured by its poetry and rhetoric, the play's message remained of little interest to its audiences. Synge, however, had the satisfaction of knowing that he had ended his writing career without abandoning his cause.

That cause was, throughout his life, the cause of liberty of the individual; he consistently attacked the moral blindness and unthinking restrictiveness of conventional religion and conventional social attitudes. He gave heroic stature to the tramp, the beggar, the dropout, and the rebel; and in his poetry he spoke with candor, humor, and vigor of matters of life and love and death which others had treated gingerly and sentimentally. He found inspiration in the difficulties of his own personal life, as well as in the predicament of the Irish countryfolk he loved and admired. He was, perhaps, because of his own personal struggle to escape from the bondage of family tradition and belief, more emotionally involved in Ireland's struggle for national identity than any other writer of his time, but, because of this personal involvement, he found himself obliged to write with a candor and vigor that made him unpopular both with his "pious relations" and with those whom he called "wilful nationalists." He achieved, however, a drama that has already long outlasted the Ireland about and in which it was written, and that has influenced the thought and writing of other playwrights and poets all over the world.

Select Bibliography

In the Shadow of the Glen (John Quinn, New York, 1904).
   An edition of fifty copies.
The Shadow of the Glen and *Riders to the Sea* (Elkin Matthews, London, 1905).
The Well of the Saints (A. H. Bullen, London, 1905).
The Well of the Saints (John Quinn, New York, 1905).
   An edition of fifty copies.
The Playboy of the Western World (Maunsel & Co., Dublin, 1907).
The Playboy of the Western World (John Quinn, New York, 1907). Act Two only. A limited edition.
The Aran Islands (Elkin Matthews, London, and Maunsel & Co., Dublin, 1907).
   Illustrated by Jack B. Yeats. A large-paper edition was issued simultaneously. Some copies bear the date 1906.
The Tinker's Wedding (Maunsel & Co., Dublin, 1908).
Poems and Translations (Cuala Press, Dublin, 1909).
   An edition of 250 copies.
Poems and Translations (John Quinn, New York, 1909).
   An edition of fifty copies.
Deirdre of the Sorrows (Cuala Press, Dublin, 1910).
   An edition of 250 copies.
Deirdre of the Sorrows (John Quinn, New York, 1910).

An edition of fifty copies, some of which were destroyed and some reissued with nine leaves of errata added.

The Works of John M. Synge (Maunsel & Co., Dublin, 1910).

Volume I: *The Shadow of the Glen, Riders to the Sea, The Tinker's Wedding, The Well of the Saints.*

Volume II: *The Playboy of the Western World, Deirdre of the Sorrows, Poems, Translations from Petrarch, Translations from Villon and others.*

Volume III: *The Aran Islands.*

Volume IV: *In Wicklow, In West Kerry, In the Congested Districts, Under Ether.*

Plays by John M. Synge (Allen & Unwin, London, 1932).

This contains some previously unpublished material from notebooks.

J. M. Synge: Translations. Edited by Robin Skelton (The Dolmen Press, Dublin, 1961).

An edition of 750 copies.

J. M. Synge: Collected Works. General Editor, Robin Skelton. (Oxford University Press, London, 1962–1968).

Volume I: Poems. Edited by Robin Skelton (1961).

Volume II: Prose. Edited by Alan Price (1966).

Volume III: Plays. Edited by Ann Saddlemyer (1968).

Volume IV: Plays. Edited by Ann Saddlemyer (1968).

This is the authorized definitive edition and contains a great deal of previously unpublished material.

BIOGRAPHY AND LETTERS

W. B. Yeats: *Synge and the Ireland of his Time* (Cuala Press, Dublin, 1911).
This contains an essay by Jack B. Yeats.
With Synge in Connemara
An edition of 350 copies.

John Masefield: John M. Synge: *A Few Personal Recollections with Biographical Notes* (Cuala Press, Dublin, 1915).
An edition of 350 copies.

Rev. Samuel Synge: *Letters to my Daughter: Memories of John Millington Synge* (Talbot Press, Dublin, 1931).

David H. Greene and Edward M. Stephens: *J. M. Synge 1871–1909* (The MacMillan Company, New York and London, 1959).
The authorized biography. (Reprinted in paperback by Collier Books in 1961.)

Lawrence Wilson (Ed): *J. M. Synge: Some Letters and Documents*
(Privately printed for the editor, 1959).
An edition of 250 copies.

Ann Saddlemyer (ed): *Synge to Mackenna: The Mature Years*
A collection of Synge's letters to Stephen Mackenna, in: Robin Skelton and David R. Clark (Eds): *Irish Renaissance* (Dolmen Press, Dublin, 1965).

Robin Skelton: *J. M. Synge and his World* (Thames & Hudson, London, 1971).

Ann Saddlemyer (Ed.): *Some Letters of John M. Synge to Lady Gregory and W. B. Yeats* (Cuala Press, Dublin 1971).

Ann Saddlemyer (Ed.): *Letters to Molly. John Millington Synge to Maire O'Neill* (Harvard University Press, 1971).

CRITICISM

Francis J. Bickley: *J.M. Synge and the Irish Dramatic Movement* (Constable, London, 1912).

Maurice Bourgeois: *John Millington Synge and the Irish Theatre* (Constable, London, 1913).

P.P. Howe: *J.M. Synge: A Critical Study* (Secker, London, 1912).

Daniel Corkery: *Synge and Anglo-Irish Literature* (Cork University Press, 1931).

L.A.G. Strong: *John Millington Synge* (Allen & Unwin, London, 1941).

Alan Price: *Synge and Anglo-Irish Drama* (Methuen, London, 1959).

Ann Saddlemyer: *J.M. Synge and Modern Comedy* (The Dolmen Press, Dublin, 1968).

Robin Skelton: *The Writings of J.M. Synge* (Thames & Hudson, London, 1971).

BIBLIOGRAPHY

Mary Pollard and Ian MacPhail: *John Millington Synge 1871–1909: A Catalogue of an Exhibition held at Trinity College Library, Dublin, on the Occasion of the Fiftieth Anniversary of his Death.* (For the friends of the Library of Trinity College, Dublin, 1959.)

This should be consulted in conjunction with an article by Ian MacPhail in *The Irish Book* for Spring 1959.